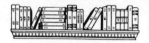 **The**

WELL-STOCKED
BOOKCASE

Seventy-Two Enduring Novels by Americans
Published Between 1926 & 1998

D1245731

FROM THE EDITORS OF
BOOK-OF-THE-MONTH CLUB

Book-of-the-Month Club
New York

Book design by The Sarabande Press

Book-of-the-Month Club
1271 Avenue of the Americas
New York, NY 10020

Printed in the United States of America

An Introductory Note to the New Edition of The Well-Stocked Bookcase

The Editorial Board of Book-of-the-Month Club decided in 1998 that it was time to revise and update this little book that was first offered on the occasion of BOMC's sixtieth anniversary in 1986. At that time, the Board selected sixty American novels, which were deemed the most important and influential fiction published during those decades, novels whose impact has endured, "novels that have changed how we Americans talk, think, write, feel and see ourselves," in the words of then editor in chief Gloria Norris. The other judges on the board at that time were Clifton Fadiman, John K. Hutchens, David Willis McCullough, Mordecai Richler, and Wilfred Sheed.

In her introduction to the first edition, Norris described how the titles were selected:

> We gathered for an informal dinner and compared lists . . . we were surprised to find that our job wasn't as easy as we thought it would be. It quickly became clear that my favorite member of my book family wasn't necessarily anyone else's favorite, that one person's "best" Bellow novel wasn't another's best Bellow. Saul Bellow's work, in fact, led to our longest and most acrimonious discussion, with champions for many different novels. Our dinner stretched on into the night, the conversation involving us in more passion, argument and acerbity than our normal luncheon meetings do.

There were off-beat favorites that produced passionate advocacy. Wilfred Sheed early nominated Budd Schulberg's *What Makes Sammy Run?* and stuck to his guns. John Hutchens spoke so enthusiastically of Conrad Richter's trilogy, *The Trees/The Fields/The Town*, that we instantly agreed. David Willis McCullough spoke up for *The Magic Christian*, armed with the determination that he would overcome our indifference. Instead, Sheed, Richler and Norris quickly matched his enthusiasm. James Gould Cozzens's well-known *By Love Possessed* was displaced by his *Guard of Honor*. Clifton Fadiman, a noted Faulkner nonenthusiast, abstained from our intense argument on which two Faulkner novels—*The Sound and the Fury* or *Absalom, Absalom!*—we should select. Some books like Jean Stafford's *The Mountain Lion* and Wallace Stegner's *Angle of Repose*, though less visible over the years, reminded us that among the best fiction there are still treasures to be discovered—or rediscovered.

Our discussions didn't end there, but continued over several other meetings. The result for each of us was what we hope will happen for all of you who read this little book—that you will find not only many of the books here that ignited your excitement when they were new, but also many that you missed and that will give you great pleasure.

The distinguished group from the mid-1980s who sifted through six decades of American novels ate and argued more than we did. Our group in the late-1990s faced a somewhat less daunting task—"only" twelve years' worth of American literature. Of course, it turns out that the decade-plus-two that takes us nearly to the close of a pivotal century has been an astoundingly fertile period for novelists. There are first and second and seventh and tenth books by giants who will stand with any in the first sixty years: Charles Frazier, Margaret Atwood, Don DeLillo, Amy Tan, Steven Millhauser, and Joyce Carol Oates. One very significant repeat appearance is made by Toni Morrison, our most recent American Nobel laureate.

Our methodology differed, as well: Private deliberations and suggestions, very personal choices, quiet (in the age of noiseless word processors—no clacking of typewriters) writing of their brief essays. As usual, I careened dangerously close to the deadline with my contributions. Others knew exactly what needed to be said in their essays and poured them out quickly, at just the right length. Still others agonized over each word, each comma, and every copy-editing suggestion.

Where, you might ask, are Richard Price, Jane Hamilton, and Annie Proulx? What about the most recent novels by John Irving, Philip Roth, and Anne Tyler? Here is where the selection process—painful, sometimes ponderous, often wrongheaded or driven by personal bias—comes into play. If we add one of these great authors, who then do we cut? Or should we bend the ground rules to pick more than a dozen new titles? Is there something magical or sacred about seventy-two? What wonderful problems to be faced with. Is there really that much superb American fiction being written? The answer is a resounding Yes!

The passionate and clearheaded pieces by our current editors remind me how many books there are yet for me to experience. Larry Shapiro opened my eyes to the prodigious talent of novelist J. F. Powers, author of *Wheat That Springeth Green*. As ever the enthusiast for quality, Victoria Skurnick puts Amy Tan's *The Joy Luck Club* in its proper position in the pantheon. If you want to learn, or remember what makes Canadian Margaret Atwood great, see Alice van Straalen's gloss on *Alias Grace*. Arthur Goldwag, who "discovered" Charles Frazier, shares his experience of reading *Cold Mountain*. And, even better than the popular TV-film adaptation, the powerful, tragicomic Armistead Maupin in his *Tales of the City* cycle is appreciated by Michael M. Moore. And our colleague Les Pockell waxes eloquently about one of the most talked-about novels of the latter half-century, *The Bonfire of the Vanities* by Tom Wolfe.

I think the result of these efforts will stimulate and in certain places even surprise you. It pleases me to be reminded why I have so much enjoyed my several years of service at BOMC. Here are snippets and insights and evidences from some of the keenest minds I have been privileged to work with.

For better or worse, by accident or design, we have chosen reading as our vocation. We approach reading not as scholars or high priests, not as literary critics or teachers, but as "common" readers who happen to have more than 150 years of editing, publishing, and writing experience among us—just in the current crop, that is; add another 200 years, at least, for the Board from 1986. (I wonder what Dorothy Parker would say if we laid out all those years from end to end, chronologically. . . .) In any case, that's a lot of years and a lot of reading. Won't you join us?

—Greg Tobin

Contributors

CLIFTON FADIMAN

ARTHUR GOLDWAG

JOHN K. HUTCHENS

DAVID WILLIS McCULLOUGH

MICHAEL M. MOORE

GLORIA NORRIS

LESLIE M. POCKELL

MORDECAI RICHLER

LARRY SHAPIRO

WILFRED SHEED

VICTORIA SKURNICK

GREG TOBIN

ALICE VAN STRAALEN

THE ACCIDENTAL TOURIST

by Anne Tyler - 1985

In her 10th novel Anne Tyler achieves the best expression yet of the consuming theme in all her work: the war between our desire for safety and for adventure. Macon Leary has the perfect job for a man pulled between these poles—he writes travel guides for people who don't want a single surprise when going to new places. In his books Macon rules out all margin for adventure, chronicling everything from where to find a Beautyrest mattress in Madrid hotels to which Tokyo restaurants carry Sweet 'n Low. Actually Macon has reason for his desperate ordering of life, for his son, Ethan, was recently killed in a senseless holdup, and he and his wife, Sarah, are separating as a fallout of their grief.

Typical of Tyler's beguilingly eccentric characters are Macon's two brothers and sister, owners of an ancient bottle-cap factory, whom he moves in with, and Macon's dog, Edward, who develops such personality problems that he has to be taken to a dog trainer, Muriel Pritchett. Divorced and the mother of an asthmatic little boy, Muriel presides over a household as loonily disorganized as the Leary family is loonily organized—one of their card games has such arcane rules that only the family can play it. The novel centers on whether Macon will return to the steady Sarah or risk himself with Muriel. That the reader cheers first for one and then the other is a measure of how honest Tyler is in working out her theme. —G. N.

ALIAS GRACE

by Margaret Atwood - 1996

When *Alias Grace* was about to be published, someone asked me whether Book-of-the-Month Club had chosen it. "Oh yes," I said, "it's a peerless book." Even for a person who has a professional supply of adjectives for recommending books, "peerless" is a rare one. It pops out when there is no real standard of comparison for a book. *Alias Grace* is utterly original.

It's the story of a murderess, told largely from her point of view. Grace Marks was in fact a notorious figure of nineteenth-century Toronto, a servant who at sixteen went to prison for the murder of both her master and his pregnant mistress. The evidence was never conclusive, and contemporary accounts portrayed Grace as either unnaturally vile or as an innocent accomplice in someone else's crime. A doctor eager to use new arts of psychological exploration visits Grace in prison, drawing from her the story of her life and the grisly events that have unhinged it. Through Grace's cell we pass into the nineteenth-century world that has shaped and judged her; its divided society, its manners and expectations. Yet the more we are enlightened, the more mysterious Grace's story, which just seems to accommodate more possibilities. The more she speaks in her stoic but winsome voice, the more perplexing the issue of her guilt. Is she or was she mad? Just who is she . . . and how much choice does she have in the matter?

Alias Grace might strike readers as too much fun for a work of art, but I suppose you don't get everything you expect even in—or especially in—a peerless book.

—A. V. S.

ALL THE KING'S MEN

by Robert Penn Warren - 1946

I suspect that if I had to pick one novel that a non-American should read to get a handle on what this country is all about, I would, after suitable qualifications and reservations, choose Robert Penn Warren's *All the King's Men*. That is not to say it is the best novel that America has produced, or even its best political novel; but its far-from-chaotic combination of idealism and cynicism, of naiveté and duplicity, of old money and power versus new, makes it an unforgettable portrait of an outsider on the make in a world full of possibilities. That is a typically American situation. So is the fact that almost every turn of the plot hinges on someone's guilty conscience.

Published in 1946 and based loosely on the political career of Louisiana's Huey Long, the novel follows both the rise to the governorship of a back-country self-educated politician named Willie Stark and the quiet disillusionment of his press agent and general gofer Jack Burden. Like many American political stories, it is a tale that begins in reform and passes through payoffs and blackmail (both subtle and not so subtle) before ending in assassination.

Sinclair Lewis, by the way, found Willie to be "a scoundrel and a saint, a booze-hoisting vulgarian and a wise and incorruptible leader of the people, a very funny fellow and somehow wistful and lost." I think the words "saint" and "incorruptible" would have surprised Willie, but he was indeed a leader of the people.

—D. W. McC.

ANGLE OF REPOSE

by Wallace Stegner - 1971

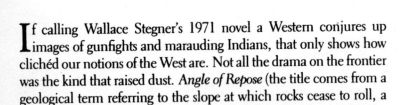

If calling Wallace Stegner's 1971 novel a Western conjures up images of gunfights and marauding Indians, that only shows how clichéd our notions of the West are. Not all the drama on the frontier was the kind that raised dust. *Angle of Repose* (the title comes from a geological term referring to the slope at which rocks cease to roll, a place of equilibrium) is a leisurely told novel of discovery and settlement, but also of acclimation and accommodation.

Set in California, Idaho, Colorado and the Dakotas, it tells of two unlikely pioneers who came West in the 1870s: Oliver Ward, a visionary mining engineer with dreams of projects that would bring civilization to the desert, and his wife, Susan, an artist whose illustrated articles about life in the West bring her a certain fame in the literary East. The narrator, their grandson Lyman Ward, a historian in his 60s deserted by his wife and suffering from cancer, lives in the family home in California. He pieces together his grandparents' story from old letters and memories of conversations with Susan when she was an old woman.

Much of the novel's richness comes from the way the past and the present feed on each other, at least in Lyman's mind. His wife's adultery helps him understand Susan's (and vice versa); his grandfather's ineffectual dreams mirror his own, and the difficulties between Lyman and his Victorian parents have echoes in the distance between Lyman and his children.

Stegner's West is a new land in which the sorrows and small happinesses of the past live on. It's a West that is not yet won.

—D. W. McC.

APPOINTMENT IN SAMARRA

by John O'Hara - 1934

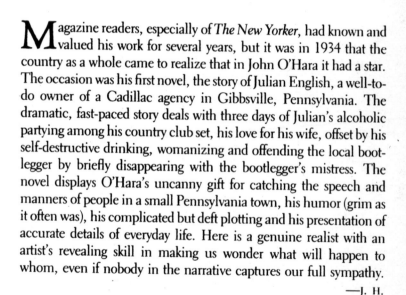

Magazine readers, especially of *The New Yorker,* had known and valued his work for several years, but it was in 1934 that the country as a whole came to realize that in John O'Hara it had a star. The occasion was his first novel, the story of Julian English, a well-to-do owner of a Cadillac agency in Gibbsville, Pennsylvania. The dramatic, fast-paced story deals with three days of Julian's alcoholic partying among his country club set, his love for his wife, offset by his self-destructive drinking, womanizing and offending the local bootlegger by briefly disappearing with the bootlegger's mistress. The novel displays O'Hara's uncanny gift for catching the speech and manners of people in a small Pennsylvania town, his humor (grim as it often was), his complicated but deft plotting and his presentation of accurate details of everyday life. Here is a genuine realist with an artist's revealing skill in making us wonder what will happen to whom, even if nobody in the narrative captures our full sympathy.

—J. H.

THE ASSISTANT

by Bernard Malamud - 1957

Set during the Depression, it is the story of Morris Bober, the quintessential Malamud Jew, a failing grocer sustained by his belief in humility and goodness. Bober's little grocery store is robbed by two men who beat up Morris badly. One day a stranger appears, asks to work in the store, and is hired by Morris over his wife's protests. This is Frank Alpine, one of the gunmen, who has returned for reasons he cannot himself understand. He helps out, but he also helps himself to cash from the till. Morris fires him, unaware that Frank has become enamored of his daughter, Helen. Actually, the little grocery, increasingly hard-pressed by a local supermarket, earns very little money. It is Helen who is doing the most to support the family. Helen has begun to respond to the assistant, but Frank just about ruins everything by forcing himself on her at one point. When Morris falls ill, Frank resumes work at the store. One day he blurts out that he was one of the robbers and Morris fires him again. But when Morris dies, a driven Frank returns to the store for a third time. Helen, who grasps that he has changed, warms to him. Frank has himself circumcised and becomes a Jew.

This Malamud novel is bound to last as a classic story of redemption and the Jewish capacity to understand suffering. —M. R.

BASTARD OUT OF CAROLINA

by Dorothy Allison - 1992

I t took a while to happen, but when readers eventually found *Bastard out of Carolina* they grabbed it, consumed it, shared it, experienced it like few books of its time. More than a "cult classic" (a term with a somewhat condescending taint), it is an ice-bright phenomenon now firmly fixed in the literary galaxy. For its in-your-face impact, I rate Dorothy Allison's first novel in the same class as *To Kill a Mockingbird* and *The Great Gatsby,* each a perfect specimen in its own right.

The writing is raw and emotional. It is not an elegant book, nor a story with a happy ending—though it provides a soaring spiritual uplift as I believe a major novel should. Ruth Anne, nicknamed Bone, gives the novel an authentic voice with a South Carolina "white trash" twang that is both harrowing and endearing. Her family is "a bunch of drunks and thieves and bastards," according to an erstwhile friend. Bone was born the bastard child of fifteen-year-old Anney Boatwright, who at twenty-one married Glen Waddell and gave Bone a stepfather. The girl plays an ever more dangerous role in a tragic triangle, which inevitably destroys the fabric of their cobbled-together family.

Like Nick Carraway, the narrator of *Gatsby,* and Scout Finch, the unforgettable voice of *Mockingbird,* Bone sees things and says things that lie at the core of our experience as human beings in the latter half of the twentieth century. She is something of a savant and a sage; and the content of her philosophy is irreligious, based on hard experience: "It wasn't God who made us like this, I thought. We'd gotten ourselves messed up on our own."

Bastard out of Carolina is a powerful, profane paean to American girlhood and motherhood—but not to apple pie. —G. T.

BECAUSE IT IS BITTER, AND BECAUSE IT IS MY HEART

by Joyce Carol Oates - 1990

There are so few good novels about race relations in America that the ones we have deserve celebration. *Because It Is Bitter, and Because It Is My Heart* is a fierce, hypnotic story of the 1950s about a black boy and a white girl whose lives cross in a terrible secret and are forever haunted. The novel's portrait of separate, unequal societies reminds me of a wistful expression often applied in the case of people who don't treat each other right. It says, in some variation: "If only they lived through some experience together, then they'd get along." Oates provides the literary equivalent of such a crucible; but she leaves the getting along to us. Occasionally-punctured segregation was the only real option in the '50s. But the novel also raises the question: How different, really, are things today?

—A. V. S.

THE BELL JAR

by Sylvia Plath - 1963

Some of the Sylvia Plath cult results undoubtedly from the romantic and tragic nature of her life, which ended with her suicide in London after the breakup of her marriage. But one need never have heard anything of Plath's life to be gripped by this powerful account of a young woman's breakdown from schizophrenia. Based on Plath's own experience as a guest editor of *Mademoiselle*, the prize for a contest that in the 1950s stimulated the daydreams of all intellectual young college women, *The Bell Jar* chronicles a gifted young woman's struggle to find herself as her love affair with a stuffy young man turns sour, as she competes with other elite young women, and as she undergoes an unsettling apprenticeship under a woman editor whose life both repels and attracts her. Feelings of loneliness and fragility overcome her and she feels descending over her a bell jar—an invisible dome sealing her off from everyone. Like Mary McCarthy's *The Group*, the novel can be enjoyed partly as a social chronicle of coming of age in a particular time, but the central figure, attempting suicide and out of contact with her world, could come from any era. *The Bell Jar* continues to radiate a powerful vision and presence.

—G. N.

BELOVED

by Toni Morrison - 1987

Beloved won the Pulitzer Prize for Fiction, and garnered some of the most ecstatic reviews of Toni Morrison's career. Set in post-Civil War Ohio, the story centers on a small clutch of characters who are related by marriage, by blood, and by the immediate and searing experience of slavery. The novel is dedicated, significantly, to "Sixty Million and more." Would that any of them might experience the words inspired by their sacrifice. Or, perhaps, they have. All that remains for the curious contemporary reader who has not read this novel is to read this novel.

Perhaps the less said the better: Toni Morrison's fifth novel (of seven to date) is so compact, so intense in its language and imagery, that it belies any attempt to embellish. *Beloved* will delight and astound and fill you with such a powerful sense of identification with its characters that you will never, I dare say, ever forget it.

—G. T.

THE BONFIRE
OF THE VANITIES

by Tom Wolfe - 1987

Tom Wolfe is not really a novelist—he's a moralist who uses prose to get his message across. Until he wrote *Bonfire of the Vanities* he had done so largely through the mechanism of corruscating magazine journalism that achieved its satirical effect as much through its jagged prose style—words used as weapons—as by its ridicule of popular icons and institutions that he felt were desecrating what remained of American culture and society. In his only previous full-length book, *The Right Stuff* (1979), Wolfe had atypically produced profiles of men—the Mercury astronauts and their predecessors—who he clearly felt were genuinely heroic. By the time *Bonfire of the Vanities* was published in 1987, its author had given up on heroes, and was ready for the apocalypse.

The original bonfire of the vanities, in fifteenth-century Florence, consumed the vain material goods of the worldly people of the City, called to purify themselves by the incendiary sermons of the monk Girolamo Savonarola. In Wolfe's book the vanities are mainly those of entitlement (privilege is not a strong enough word). Ostensibly the narrative centers around a putatively aristocratic Yale graduate/Park Avenue/bond trader named Sherman McCoy, a self-designated Master of the Universe, whose seemingly impregnable position in life is actually so fragile that it doesn't survive a missed exit on the way back to the city from Kennedy Airport. (One of Wolfe's great riffs on Sherman's vulnerability is his anguished and painstaking calculation that he can find no way to live within his million-dollar annual income.) As Sherman

12

attempts to extricate himself from an entangling chain of lies and self-deception, his descent is abetted by lawyers, journalists, clergymen, politicians, socialites, and the wretched refuse of the teeming shore that once stood as a beacon to the oppressed of Europe. In Wolfe's hands and through his words, New York City becomes a sort of Inferno, a dark maelstrom of dysfunction in which no adult citizen emits any sort of hopeful illumination. Like some landscape by Hieronymus Bosch, *Bonfire of the Vanities* casts a baleful light on human endeavor in the person of innumerable sinners, some weak and defeated, others greedy and ravening, devouring each other as they are devoured.

Paradoxically, reading this fulminating narrative, inhabiting the consciousness of these cowards and villains, becomes an exhilarating experience for the reader, for rather than identifying with any character, as in conventional fiction, we tend to see things from the author's imperious viewpoint, pointing with scorn as he does at the snivelling Sherman and his companions beneath us in the abyss. Only when Sherman finds all that he values stripped from him (though he is surely no Job-like figure!) does the author deign to offer him a shred of dignity; as he prepares to confront his new life alone and friendless, Sherman seems to find his self respect at last. Perhaps this is Wolfe's final moral: only when you realize that your presumed entitlements are as ashes can you begin to recover your sense of yourself as a human being, and part of a worthy society. Of course, *Bonfire of the Vanities* made its author a very wealthy man, but presumably the principle still applies.   —L. M. P.

BURR

by Gore Vidal - 1973

It may come as a shock at first to hear George Washington described as a wide-bottomed, dull-eyed real estate man and Jefferson as a towering monument of deceit. But these descriptions also remind us that the Founding Fathers were not yet sacred cows in their own lifetimes (although Washington sounds as if he was rather built like one) and that consequently their writings, including the Constitution itself, were not the immutable scriptures they have since become, but highly charged political documents of the moment, still open to debate and defiance.

The speaker is Aaron Burr, and the point of the above characterizations is that he is a New Yorker talking about Virginians. Burr, our narrator, has never understood how the Virginians had so easily swiped the Revolution and run with it, getting the early presidencies and leaving everyone else scrambling. Burr was later accused of trying to build his own empire in other parts of the continent, but his fellow New Yorker Alexander Hamilton nursed similar wild schemes: both were reacting to a United States that seemed to them to have become simply an extension, or larger version, of Virginia. That they wound up dueling *each other* may be a testament to their frustration.

In the person of Burr, Gore Vidal has found his doppelgänger, and the perfect 18th- and 19th-century spokesman for his own views—which are, as always, tart, curmudgeonly and very witty. But if one suspects that the author is simply using Burr, I gather that a look at Vidal's period sources will put one's mind at rest. As in his majestic

Lincoln, Vidal's skill at imitation makes it impossible to tell which quotations are real and which are made up. They are all in the same key.

Burr's story is told against a backdrop of 1830s politics, which also gives us a chance to see how the Founders' dreams worked out in practice and, not incidentally, to note how easily Vidal moves between periods, completely at home in our past, and perhaps the only historical novelist we have to put up with pride against the great Europeans.

—W. S.

CATCH-22

by Joseph Heller - 1961

C*atch-22* was published more than a quarter of a century ago. That's hard to believe. Both its title and its text have kept it alive. The words "catch-22" are now not only part of the language but part of our consciousness. As the human race drifts (or so it sometimes appears) into a no-win situation, the phrase seems to acquire increasing prophetic power. And the book itself has plenty of survival value. It's not exactly a war novel, as *The Naked and the Dead* is a war novel, but the War generated it. Joseph Heller transformed his experience— 60 combat missions as a bombardier—into a stunningly original protest against war, using nonrealistic techniques with remarkable success. *Catch-22* is funny and serious, crazy and grimly sane. Its anti-hero Captain John Yossarian may prove to have a life of his own, like Babbitt or Père Goriot.

—C. F.

THE CATCHER IN THE RYE

by J. D. Salinger - 1951

The Catcher in the Rye was the Book-of-the-Month Club's mid-summer Selection in 1951. Since then it has been read by millions and is still being read all over the world. The Club's Editorial Board, be assured, did not foresee that it would at once become a kind of scripture for a whole generation. Today Holden Caulfield is part of the population of our minds, but back in 1951 he was a total surprise. Still, I think we recognized the book's quality—not always easy to do when an author is virtually unknown and especially when he opens up new paths in style and sensibility. Our report to our members called J. D. Salinger "brilliant" and then at once qualified the judgment: "one may be brilliant and have little to say." It continued: "Brilliance is born merely of a smooth reflecting surface. Mr. Salinger, however . . . has polish *and* depth. His book arouses our admiration—but, more to the point, it starts flowing in us the clear springs of pity, understanding and affectionate laughter." And for 36 years that has generally been the response to the adolescent Holden Caulfield, with his unsatisfied thirst for goodness, his fierce, rebellious, confused passion to be an individual.

The Catcher in the Rye, when it first appeared, seemed to voice its period with almost perilous perfection. But the voice is still strong. There must be Holden Caulfields in every generation, and perhaps in all of us.

—C. F.

COLD MOUNTAIN

by Charles Frazier - 1997

Two years after its publication, with millions of copies sold and a movie on the way, *Cold Mountain* has become something of a cultural phenomenon. But Charles Frazier's good fortune is our loss, because one of the greatest pleasures his book affords is its amazing capacity to surprise. Reading it in manuscript—before the glowing reviews, before the author's television appearances, before its inexorable climb up the bestseller lists—I was overwhelmed by the simultaneous sense that it had always existed and that it was something entirely new.

Frazier's language, biblically plain, but rich with the precise and sometimes archaic diction of hunting, husbandry, and natural history, is entirely his own. And if his themes are familiar—the horrors of war, the struggle to wrest one's living out of the ground, love between man and woman—that is because they are what animates so much of the world's literature. *Cold Mountain* may be the flavor-of-the-month now, but I'm convinced that it will endure. It has the heft and feel of a classic. —A. G.

THE COUNTERLIFE

by Philip Roth - 1987

The major themes in the novels of Philip Roth are not very difficult to name—sexuality, being Jewish, his search for his best self, and a somewhat ambivalent longing for the unknown (often, less fancily, merely a shiksa girlfriend). But nowhere in Roth's work are these themes as brilliantly reckoned with as in *The Counterlife*. And they are joined by a joyous literary innovation that is a departure from his earlier novels.

Not even in the masterful *Portnoy's Complaint* did Roth make the imaginative leaps that enable him to take this tale of two brothers, Nathan and Henry Zuckerman, and stir the family pot with alternating lives, alternative realities. Henry, the successful dentist father of three and husband of one, is rendered impotent by his heart medication. Does he undergo surgery that kills him? Does he survive to move to Israel and become a zealot? Is he a good father, a terrible father, a fanatical simpleton, an inspired acolyte? He is, in Roth's magical sleight of hand, all of the above.

Capping the imaginative and the witty is the brilliant: very rarely has anyone—writer, politician, citizen—captured on the page every possible argument about the state of Israel. The country comes alive not just as a national hotbed, but as the spirit of everything Jews feel about Jews. If the Roth of *When She Was Good* was a normal self-hating young man, and the Roth of Portnoy a smart-aleck genius, the Roth of *The Counterlife* is a fully-formed adult who offends and explains and parses and praises, and leaves us feeling filled beyond measure.   —V. S.

THE DAY OF THE LOCUST

by Nathanael West - 1939

The Day of the Locust is still the best novel ever written about Hollywood. A surreal, even Hogarthian novel about Hollywood flotsam, people who never cut a deal in the Polo Lounge or made anybody's A list. A landlady whose hobby is funerals, a cocksure dwarf, a dying vaudeville comic, a juicy little extra, a repulsive child actor and his even more horrific mom—all seen through the eyes of Tod Hackett, a lost bookkeeper out of Iowa, hoping for a career as a set designer.

"West is an original comic poet," wrote Edmund Wilson. *"The Day of the Locust* has scenes of extraordinary power," said F. Scott Fitzgerald.

Nathanael West, who gave us another satirical classic, *Miss Lonelyhearts*, died almost unknown in 1940. He was, to my mind, one of the finest American writers of the 1930s.   —M. R.

DEATH COMES FOR
THE ARCHBISHOP

by Willa Cather - 1927

Her earlier novels—including *O Pioneers!*, *My Antonía* and *A Lost Lady*—established Willa Cather as a writer of the first order. One became further convinced of her artistry with the publication of this book, in which her style and grace were again apparent. One was slightly surprised, too—for here she is not only a storyteller but a historian. This time she went into the past, the mid-19th century, and faraway, to the American Southwest, to tell a story of two missionary French priests who brought sanctity to a wild and lawless area. As vicar apostolic of New Mexico, Father Latour makes his precarious way to Santa Fe in 1851, arriving at a beautiful but wild land where his priests are sometimes murdered and other times succumb to vice themselves. Over the next 40 years he and his associate from the seminary, Father Vaillant, labor to bring the faith to the Southwest.

The book is frequently anecdotal and seemingly casual, but only superficially so, in its narrative form. Spanish colonial history, Mexican customs, the rituals and legends of the Indian pueblos are plausibly re-created. In one lively interlude the famous frontiersman Kit Carson becomes an unlikely partner of the two missionaries. This is an engrossing return to a place in our past that has been neglected.

—J. H.

DELTA WEDDING

by Eudora Welty - 1946

"Nothing short of wonderful," declared Hamilton Basso in *The New Yorker* of this novel. "I find it difficult to determine how much of my distaste for Eudora Welty's new book is dislike of its literary manner and how much is resistance to the culture out of which it grows and which it describes so fondly," huffed Diana Trilling in *The Nation*. The two reactions sum up the dilemma of the Southern writer faced with national critics: praised and sometimes overpraised, on the one hand, for the exoticism of their fiction; condemned, on the other hand, for not blending social criticism into this exotic, highly personal fiction. Readers who recently discovered Welty for the first time in her memoir, *One Writer's Beginnings*, should delight in this fictional story of Mississippi childhood set in the same period.

Nine-year-old Laura McRaven, after her mother's death, travels alone for a wedding at the Delta plantation of her idolized cousins, the Fairchilds. Their daughter Dabney is marrying the plantation overseer, and a great crowd of cousins, aunts, great-aunts and uncles assembles. Uncle George's wife, Robbie (like the overseer, a person of lesser social distinction than the Fairchilds), is painfully absent, for she has grown tired of feeling that her husband loves his family more than her. Dabney herself is torn between her new married love and her love for family. Laura, so newly orphaned, idolizes their family unity, and the novel explores a continuing Welty theme—the strengths and weaknesses of Southern family ties. Welty's ear for speech and her lyric prose add to the novel's beauties.   —G. N.

EDWIN MULLHOUSE
THE LIFE AND DEATH OF AN AMERICAN WRITER, 1943-1954, BY JEFFREY CARTWRIGHT

by Steven Millhauser - 1972

It's often the books you don't expect to like that knock you off your feet. Consider *Edwin Mullhouse*, which I read last year to see what the fuss was about and because I was tired of saying no, I haven't read it. Most of the characters in *Edwin Mullhouse* are children. Early on I noticed a covert quality about them that brought to mind *Lord of the Flies*, although this novel is spookier than *Lord of the Flies* and a thousand times more ingenious. It shows normality and oddness coexisting in childhood, sometimes so intermingled in one child that it's hard to say what is normal until something terrible happens. The portrait of a typical American family of the late 1940s and early 1950s, the Mullhouses, is both achingly nostalgic and oddly off-kilter, reminding us that every family's rituals are both familiar and unique. Most memorably there's the story of Edwin Mullhouse's unrequited love for his second grade classmate Rose Dorn, which seems to incorporate the ingredients of every love story ever written, but transformed into something bizarre, comical, heartbreaking, and oddly beautiful. And there are three friendships between Edwin Mullhouse and other boys, each recognizable, each disquieting, as if those of us who have grown to adulthood are glimpsing something so distant that it has become foreign.

So far as I know, no one writing about this book has ever given away the surprise of its ending. And I won't be the first.   —L. S.

A FAN'S NOTES

by Frederick Exley - 1968

When *A Fan's Notes* landed in the sixties, it hit town like an unexplained chunk of meteor. The book was dazzling in an unearthly sort of way—but what exactly was it? It seemed too inventively funny and fantastical to be a memoir, but it was also much too real and painful to be anything else: *some*one had lived through this phantasmagoria, and not just in his mind.

Anyway, when in doubt we call them novels, and *A Fan's Notes* quickly became a cult one. Its central image, of a man who can find order and peace in this crazy world only by watching New York Giant football games, seemed to strike a chord with many Americans—and not just football fanciers: it seems that our oases from chaos lurk in strange places.

The Exley character is torn to psychic shreds by two characteristically American drives which tug at him like runaway horses. The first drive is for pure excellence and superiority of spirit; the other is for success on any terms at all, the trashier the better. Thus Exley the Excellent, the super-esthete, can look down his nose at practically everything with a satiric scorn worthy of a grown-up Holden Caulfield, while little Freddy the success worshipper is overwhelmed and unmanned by just about anything that smacks even faintly of success, and to hell with excellence.

At the center of this muddle stalks the unlikely figure of Frank Gifford, the New York Giant football star. It seems that Gifford used to be the King of the Campus when he and Exley attended Southern Cal back in the 1940s; later when our hero makes it to New York, he finds that Gifford is King there, too. Yet Exley the snob can find nothing *wrong* with him, nothing to sneer at, and his soul seems, well almost, at rest.

But only until the final whistle blows of a Sunday, at which point the war is on again. Exley's abiding torment is that he sees everything with the lucidity of genuine madness and responds to it with the barely-controlled hysteria that such lucidity demands. To dim this blinding vision, he tends to drown his cerebrum in rivers of booze, to the point where *A Fan's Notes* occasionally reminds me of *Under the Volcano* played as a two-reel comedy.

Because finally, the author's manic desire to outrun his demons through the course of a wonderfully farcical career is at least as funny and heart-lifting as it is pathetic. And at the end, the reader may feel less downcast than weirdly elated—on the possible grounds that, if this poor sonofabitch can make it through a whole book, anybody can and that if the real Exley ever truly craved excellence and recognition this much for himself, *A Fan's Notes* must have brought him both in ungovernable quantities.   —W. S.

A FAREWELL TO ARMS

by Ernest Hemingway - 1929

Almost 60 years after its first appearance, is there anything fresh or even interesting to say about Ernest Hemingway's most lyrical, most purely beautiful novel? Probably not. I don't think I want to find out. I haven't dared to re-read it, for I prefer to retain unchanged my memory of the impression it made on me and my generation. It made war real for us as no history book had ever done. And though we later learned to question Hemingway's view of women, it offered us a love story whose romanticism seemed authentic and moving. The famous style had not yet become mannered; one didn't feel or hear the master's file working away at the sentences. The aggressive masculinity was still moderately expressed.

And so, asked to name Hemingway's finest novel, I'd take A Farewell to Arms. Certainly, for me at least, World War I produced no better work of fiction. It lingers in the mind like music. Somehow, when I call it back, all the critical wars waged against Hemingway during his life and after his death fade into irrelevance. True, it is by his short stories that he will live; they changed everything. But in A Farewell to Arms his art, the cruxes of his own life and his passionate feeling for the tragic faces of love and war were held in delicate suspension as in none of his other longer works. —C. F.

A FLAG FOR SUNRISE

by Robert Stone - 1981

Reflecting on some of the twisted, unhappy characters he has created, Robert Stone once remarked: "We haven't accepted the moral dimensions of what's happening around us, and the effect is a kind of numbness. People begin to act unpredictably, sometimes spectacularly, and begin to surprise themselves in the face of their extreme conditions." Stone may develop into a classic American expositor of these extreme conditions.

A *Flag for Sunrise*, the Club's Selection for January, 1982, sticks in the mind as a good example of Stone's almost apocalyptic vision of our time. Its background, an "imaginary" Central American republic, and its grim view of the human condition recall *Nostromo*. But Conrad's code of honor and duty has been replaced here by moral anarchy. After all (see Stone's remarkable earlier book *Dog Soldiers*), we are post-Vietnam.

A *Flag for Sunrise* brews a desperate mix of violence, drugs, crazy insurrectionists, a radical nun, an alcoholic priest, homosexual double agents and similar ingredients to produce a novel whose bleakness of outlook is relieved only by its intensity. Stone started as a counterculture man and by now he may have outgrown it. But he has retained some of the counterculture's sense of the historical divide on which we stand. The old values, for him, are played out; new ones are not yet visible. He is an expert on lost souls. —C. F.

FROM HERE TO ETERNITY

by James Jones - 1951

Although usually classified as a war novel, *From Here to Eternity* ends just as World War II begins. Never mind: it is a war novel. The peacetime army that James Jones dissects so powerfully would soon be a wartime army, and its future is written in its present like a dog tag. The sadism and decency, the rivalries and friendships of the NCOs and dogfaces will next find them doing duty in Guadalcanal (Jones's own port of call in his later novel, *The Thin Red Line*); while the pettiness and myopia of the officers receives its answer when the bombs drop on an undefended Pearl Harbor. It is a tribute to Jones's mesmeric intensity that he makes this bombing seem more like the private climax of his novel than a public event. The bombing of course took place on a Sunday; by then we know exactly how these guys spend Saturday night and how they feel on Sunday morning: some of them could probably hear bombs going off even before they arrived.

But the central story of Captain Holmes and Private Prewitt is the real parable of that day. Prewitt is a talented boxer who once nearly killed a man and wants no further part of it; but Holmes needs him for his regimental team, which is at once his pride and joy and his claim to status in an otherwise motionless army. When Prewitt refuses, the captain pours all his finest military energies into breaking him. To hell with the outside world (which never enters the book—or the peacetime army—anyway); he will get this one man. Prewitt finally proves unbreakable, at least spiritually. But as the war begins and the captain tries to gather his fuddled wits about him, Prewitt is dead, and his unit will have to fight its battles without the help of the finest and bravest soldier it ever had. Prewitt, playing taps on his bugle for the last time, bids an eloquent farewell to peace and its discontents, and to an unforgettable novel. —w. s.

GEEK LOVE

by Katherine Dunn - 1988

Geek Love offers yet another confirmation of Tolstoy's dictum that every unhappy family is unhappy in its own way, but one measure of the distance literature has traveled since *Anna Karenina* is that the unhappy Binewski family consists largely of a group of carnival freaks. Tolstoy's example also teaches us that short titles can have a powerful impact, but this one derives its effect from incongruity as well; what exactly is geek love? In fact, what is a geek? A classic geek is a carny performer who does odd and disgusting things to attract an audience, like eating lightbulbs and razor blades, or biting off a live chicken's head. The book's title derives from the caption to a graphic pen-and-ink portrayal of this latter act drawn by the narrator's 20-year-old daughter, a stunning medical illustrator/stripper named Miranda whose only physical abnormality—a curling tail protruding from her spine—impels a critical plot element of this phantasmagorical thriller.

Geek is a term sometimes understandably conflated with freak, but in general carnival freaks don't have to perform; their physical oddity is sufficient to guarantee their livelihood. Perhaps the most famous freaks in American culture—besides Barnum's Original Siamese Twins—are those that populated Tod Browning's classic movie of that title. The most unnerving quality of the movie was that the actors were real freaks who were placed in their own fictional society within a carnival. Their dramatized relationships are reminiscent of what we encounter in more naturalistic drama, if not the real world, but the tragic consequences are intensified and made horrifying by the distorted bodies of the cast, heightened by angular shadows and unexpected camera angles. In *Geek Love* Katherine Dunn has created her world out of words alone, but it is just as compelling as the one in *Freaks,* and even more believable, despite its surrealistic, and in some cases supernatural, components, because the voice that describes that world and tells its story is one of the most powerful and persuasive in modern fiction: the resonant, modulated, nuanced voice of Olympia Binewski, a tiny, twisted, bald albino hunchback who is desperately trying to reconcile her past and her present.

Olympia, like all the Binewskis, holds the world of norms in contempt; being a geek is to her a rare and treasured kind of uniqueness. And by the end of the book, enrapt and presumably normal readers may themselves feel somehow incomplete without a tail or some other token of the extraordinary bonds of kinship among the geeks. Katherine Dunn's ultimate triumph in this unforgettable novel is to have transcended limitations of form to reveal the essential qualities of love and beauty that make us all more or less human.
                                                                    —L. M. P.

GONE WITH THE WIND

by Margaret Mitchell - 1936

In one of his essays T. S. Eliot assesses Kipling's qualities and importance as a poet. After reading it we conclude that, though one would never mention Keats and Kipling in the same breath, it would be wrong to deny the latter his special genius, a magnificent general availability. There are very few public poets to match him.

Similarly, compared with the number of great "literary" novelists, there are very few great popular novelists. By "popular" one does not mean trashy or venal or ephemeral. Great popular novelists are absolutely honest, absolutely uncompromising in their view of life, absolutely faithful to their conception of art. Margaret Mitchell is such a one.

Gone With the Wind has shown its power to reach (in the deepest sense of the word) tens of millions of readers in more than 35 countries—and to keep on reaching them for half a century. As we meditate on its sweeping narrative and its outsize characters, we are led to reject the word "stereotype" and substitute the word "archetype." Scarlett O'Hara, whom we admire almost against our will, reflects the most primal of our instinctive drives: the will to survive. Her appeal is akin to that of Robinson Crusoe. She and Rhett Butler—and also the very different Melanie and Ashley—embody deep-rooted human dreams and desires, not all of them a credit to our nature. *Gone With the Wind* is not a great novel, but it is a great story.

When our judges made it the July, 1936, Selection, they were merely acknowledging slightly in advance what millions of readers were quick to recognize.

—C. F.

THE GRAPES OF WRATH

by John Steinbeck - 1939

Younger Americans may read this book not so much as a novel as a work of history: a history of a period that was possibly the most terrifying one that our nation has known since the Civil War. John Steinbeck's vision of the Depression is embodied in the story of a Dust Bowl family of farm folks, the Joads, migrating to what they hope will be security in California. Their misery and misadventures are appalling, including the death of Grampa, then Granma, the loss of a son, persecution and exploitation by California farmers and police and the stillbirth of a daughter's baby.

Despised by local inhabitants as "Okies," or tramps, they carry on as best they can until they achieve a form of survival. The hallmark of the book is indignation, and such is the author's anger at the social cruelty of the period that his characters are profane and rough as well as tender and understanding. Yet, as in several of Steinbeck's preceding novels—notably, *Of Mice and Men*, *Tortilla Flat* and *In Dubious Battle*—the book has a place for humor as well as bitterness, which is by way of saying that it has the virtue of wholeness. —J. H.

GUARD OF HONOR

by James Gould Cozzens - 1948

Set within the space of three days in 1943 at an air force base in Florida, this novel is so rich in plot and detail that one feels as if one had spent a month experiencing it. Thanks to James Gould Cozzens narrative gift, which he had been developing with increasing maturity in his previous work, the action flows freely from one crisis to another—an airplane accident that hospitalizes a black flyer, a racial conflict that threatens to become a riot, a quarrel between the military and the citizenry of the town, the terrible fate of a company of parachutists whose ill-timed leap sends them to disaster. Much of the book's success, one realizes, derives from the Cozzens style: its quiet, unemphatic tone makes believable events that might have had a melodramatic flamboyance. A first-rate writer was at his best here.

—J. H.

THE HEART IS A
LONELY HUNTER

by Carson McCullers - 1940

oming from a young woman of 23, this first novel appeared like a
thunderbolt to American readers. They were intrigued by a
surprisingly mature and accomplished novel as well as by blown-up
photographs in bookstores of the author—who appeared to be a
girlish 16-year-old with bangs and plump cheeks.

Set in Georgia, where the narrowness of a small town accentuates
the lonely yearnings of its "hunters," the book's characters include
the sensitive, tomboyish Mick, who is drawn to spill out her dreams
and ambitions to the town's mysterious deaf-mute, John Singer.
Mesmerized in the same way are a café owner, a drifter and a black
doctor. Mick springs from a long tradition of rebellious adolescents in
American fiction, from Tom Sawyer to Holden Caulfield, but Carson McCullers' story also demonstrates remarkable perception about
the loneliness of the human heart and the societal indifference and
hypocrisy that deepen it. Richard Wright in *The New Republic*
acclaimed her "astonishing humanity that enables a white writer, for
the first time in Southern fiction, to handle Negro characters with as
much ease and justice as those of her own race." Her narrative skill
and her polished prose are equally astonishing.   —G. N.

HEAVEN'S MY DESTINATION

by Thornton Wilder - 1935

During the grim 1930s, Thornton Wilder was contemptuously dismissed by the American Left as a Europeanized fop who couldn't write about his own people. This book is his answer to them—certainly not the one they expected or wanted, but one of the most American books ever written all the same. George Brush is a holy fool for Christ rather than for Marx. He is also a traveling salesman, and Wilder salutes the oldest of American jokes by actually having him succumb to a farmer's daughter. But this is his only sin. Otherwise he barges around the lower depths of the boondocks trying to do good, but mostly just getting in people's hair or alarming them, and occasionally causing vast and unforeseeable damage. (The resemblance to Woodrow Wilson's foreign policy may not be entirely unintentional.) George even tries to make cumbersome amends to the farmer's daughter, to her untold irritation.

Yet for all his blunders, which can be hilarious (he mistakes a brothel for a family mansion, complete with a wonderful mother and lovely daughters, and treats them all accordingly), the world is a better place for having him around. "America is great," wrote Alexis de Tocqueville, "because its people are good." "God," wrote another Frenchman, "writes straight with crooked lines." George Brush is a walking, stumbling and tripping proof of both propositions, and *Heaven's My Destination* is, to my mind, Thornton Wilder's best, and most *unexpected* book.

—W. S.

INVISIBLE MAN

by Ralph Ellison - 1952

Today American literature by black writers is alive and well. The nonblack audience has learned (and high time, too) to judge a work of art by a black writer as it would any other. But when *Invisible Man* appeared, this was hardly the case. Today Ralph Ellison's nightmare story of the life of a young Southern black man, exploited by both the white and the black establishments, is almost a classic. But 35 years ago it had to make its way against white narrow-mindedness, against the majority's tendency to avert its eyes.

It is not a "protest" novel, except insofar as it protests against the de-individualizing forces that work to make us all invisible men. Though rooted in black experience, it can now be judged on its merits as a novel among other novels. Many believe it to be the finest work of fiction produced by a black writer. But that is like saying that *The Ambassadors* is one of the finest novels ever written by an upper-middle-class white expatriate American. The simple fact is that *Invisible Man* is a notable addition to 20th-century American literature.

—C. F.

THE JOY LUCK CLUB

by Amy Tan - 1989

When you make a living as a book editor, you read thousands of titles. Generally you like a book or you don't, recommend it to friends if you do, and quickly go on to the next one. Rarely do you encounter that magical life-changing feeling a good book can bring (one that children really do experience any number of times).

So why, I've asked myself many times, is *The Joy Luck Club* such a special pleasure for me? Not such a mystery really for a first-generation daughter who knew how it felt to hear a mother speak the wrong language, wear the wrong clothes, pointedly disdain the norms from which I so desperately wanted to be indistinguishable.

Amy Tan's stories of the four Chinese-born mothers and their upwardly mobile American daughters are fascinating; the mothers at war with their society; the daughters at war with their mothers; both generations holding back the best of themselves from each other yet giving utterly to the reader.

My mother had her secrets as these Chinese mothers do, secrets that drew you closer and held you at arm's length at the same time. China, Poland, mothers, daughters. All the same really.   —V. S.

THE LAST HURRAH

by Edwin O'Connor - 1956

With Edwin O'Connor's first important novel it was apparent that a major new American writer had arrived. The book was and is of special interest to New England readers, since its major character, Frank Skeffington, is clearly suggested by James Michael Curley, the fabulous Boston mayor earlier in this century whom reformers abhorred and the public adored. But readers everywhere in America will be entertained by this tale of a lovable rascal's final campaign. A politician and demagogue clearly roguish in his dealings with office-hungry colleagues? He surely is—and also a moving orator, a generous, witty, charming man who accomplished for his Irish-American constituents benefits they would not otherwise have obtained. Some critics found the book overly sentimental. But most of them saw it as a historic portrait of a political era.   —J. H.

THE LATE GEORGE APLEY

by John P. Marquand - 1937

John P. Marquand's subtle satire of late 19th- and early 20th-century Boston is still his most appealing novel. Its picture of that city—its culture, its class distinctions, its virtues and its failings—are recaptured in the person of the book's title character. That Brahmin world of Apley's would go on and on, would it not? After all, his ancestors for two centuries had been Harvard alumni, Beacon Hill elitists, forever secure.

For the most part, Apley behaves the part of Brahmin ordained for him, whether that means joining the Hasty Pudding Club at Harvard, apprenticing in business (which his Uncle William advises him he is unsuited for, causing George to spend his life profitably caring for other people's investments), quietly paying off his father's mistress to avoid public scandal, and, when he realizes the threat of the up-and-coming Irish, conducting a civilized defense with the "Save Boston Association." Yet one youthful love affair comes back as ammunition in his enemies' hands. Through it all he remains a decent, generous man.

It was Marquand's feat to have been at once an ironic, penetrating realist and a sympathetic annalist. He was of that school which does not set out to prove anything but rather to describe and present. His work has its lasting attraction.　　　　—J. H.

LIBRA

by Don DeLillo - 1988

I f Lee Harvey Oswald had never been born, Don DeLillo, America's poet laureate of paranoia, might have had to invent him.

November 22, 1963, that ghastly moment in Dallas when the visible embodiment of the American Dream and the nightmare of the Cold War converged, that magnetic north for everything shadowy and duplicitous that was ever done in the name of democracy, emerges from the pages of *Libra* as both a primal, metaphysical mystery and the culmination of an all-too-human comedy.

DeLillo offers up his own theory about the Kennedy assassination, and with its blend of contingency and conspiracy, criminal cunning and grandiose delusion, misplaced idealism and political rage, it's as plausible as anything else that you're likely to read about it. But Don DeLillo is a novelist, first and foremost, not a detective, not a historian, and what makes his book so memorable are its literary qualities: the vigor and tautness of its prose; the demotic precision and jagged rhythms of its dialogue; its almost palpable evocation of time and place; the multidimensionality, sheer believability, and pathos of even its supernumerary characters and, most of all, the hallucinatory improbability and tragic inevitability that propels them outside of themselves and into history.

Libra is a masterpiece.

—A. G.

LIE DOWN IN DARKNESS

by William Styron - 1952

Another precocious Southern novel that took the public by storm, published when the author was only 27. William Styron's lyrical, metaphor-strewn prose took off from Faulkner but assumed its own distinctiveness and quickly established his own vision of a Southern family. Milton Loftis is a charming, weak man who leisurely practices law in Port Warwick, a seaport in tidewater Virginia. He and his wife, Helen, have slowly become estranged, and she uses the tragedy of a retarded daughter, Maudie, as well as Milton's philandering to feed her own tight-lipped martyrdom.

But her real anger and coldness are directed against their beautiful daughter Peyton, whom Milton idolizes and for whom, as the novel develops, he is revealed to have incestual longings. The efforts of the family to love and heal each other, Milton's selfishness, Helen's "Christian" self-destructiveness, and the poignant, intense life of Peyton, who tries to escape into marriage in New York, are told in a complex narrative. The title is drawn from Sir Thomas Browne's *Urn-Burial*: "Therefore it cannot be long before we lie down in darkness, and have our light in ashes."   —G. N.

LIGHT IN AUGUST

by William Faulkner - 1932

With William Faulkner, it is essential to start out with the right book. Until you get used to the special music of the "Dixie Cannonball" (as Flannery O'Connor once called him), reading him can be like getting lost in a dense Mississippi Delta fog. Hence the appropriateness, even down to the title, of *Light in August*—a vivid, fast-gaited and above all *accessible* novel which makes the others a lot easier to enjoy when you come to them.

Faulkner's concern here is with the outcasts of the old Jim Crow South, the white trash and mulattoes and unidentifiable drifters who have no niche in society but have as a consequence the perverse freedom to move about at will and, alternately, to help, and prey on, each other. The protagonist, Joe Christmas, is a half-caste bastard who can pass for white, most of the time. In his restless travels (Joe always seems to be on the run even when he's not), one two-part question follows him like a curse: Should I tell them I'm black, and suppose I don't tell them and they find out anyway? The ramifications of this question shape his destiny almost totally, just as race has shaped his whole region, while giving the reader a gaudy, haunting picture of the low-life South and its range of attitudes and experiences, unavailable from any source other than the Old Master himself.   —W. S.

LITTLE BIG MAN

by Thomas Berger - 1964

Few contemporary novelists have given me as much pleasure as Thomas Berger. He is an original. He is fun. A writer of the absurd to be cherished. I have devoured all four of his Reinhart novels, which I happily recommend: *Crazy in Berlin, Reinhart in Love, Vital Parts* and *Reinhart's Women*. I also hugely enjoyed *Sneaky People* and *Neighbors*.

But Berger is at his outlandish, hilarious best, I think, in *Little Big Man*, a novel of the dirty Old West as seen through the eyes of 111-year-old Jack Crabb, sole white survivor of Custer's Last Stand.

Crabb is a man of many parts. He has lost a white wife to the Indians and an Indian wife to the whites. He fought with the Cheyenne and later defected to the U.S. Army. He has worked as a muleskinner, buffalo hunter and scout. Among his beautifully realized companions are such Old West notables as Chief Old Lodge Skins, Wild Bill Hickok, Wyatt Earp, General Custer and Calamity Jane. The upshot is a marvelously funny, picaresque novel, one of the best ever written about the Old West.   —M. R.

LOLITA

by Vladimir Nabokov - 1958

It is almost 30 years since the first appearance of Vladimir Nabokov's *Lolita*. The fuss has had time to die down, and today only the uncultivated mind would agree with the earnest critic who, back in 1958, condemned it as "very literary pornography." Call it parody, call it comedy, call it a send-up of the picaresque and the horrible—but pornography, however elegant, it is not.

The theme—a grown man's obsessive passion for a 12-year-old girl—has been treated by other serious writers. The situation is by no means infrequent in real life. What counts is the Nabokovian handling, the comic genius operating on the trashy landscape of *Lolita's* mind and on the junk-America that she and Humbert Humbert traverse.

A study of perversion and of grotesque crime, *Lolita* (like so many of Nabokov's wonderful fictions) rides on an undercurrent of subtextual commentary on the nature of literary art. In this sense it recalls much of the work of Wallace Stevens.

In any event, it is almost surely Nabokov's masterpiece, though some would advance the claims of that even more intricate fable *Pale Fire*.

—C. F.

THE LONELY PASSION OF
JUDITH HEARNE

by Brian Moore - 1956

A t times it seems to me that what my generation of novelists does best, celebrating itself, is also discrediting. Too often, I think, it is we who are the fumblers, the misfits, *but unmistakably lovable*, intellectual heroes of our very own fictions, triumphant in our vengeful imaginations as we never were in actuality. Only a few contemporaries—say, Brian Moore—live up to what I once took to be the novelist's primary moral responsibility, which is to be the loser's advocate. To tell us what it's like to be a feckless Irish immigrant adrift in Montreal (*The Luck of Ginger Coffey*), a timorous schoolmaster (*The Feast of Lupercal*), or Judith Hearne.

The Lonely Passion of Judith Hearne, Moore's first novel, was a tour de force. He managed to get deep inside the skin of a pinched, middle-aged spinster living in a Belfast boardinghouse. A secret tippler, she weaves a desperate romantic fantasy round one of the other lodgers, who is only after her money. Out of this unpromising material Moore hammered out a compulsively readable novel. Astringent, compassionate, but resolutely unsentimental.   —M. R.

LOOK HOMEWARD, ANGEL

by Thomas Wolfe - 1929

It sometimes seems that the only work of Thomas Wolfe's that's read these days is the title of his fourth novel, *You Can't Go Home Again*. What sportswriter, columnist or run-of-the-mill newspaper sage could stay in business if he couldn't at least once a year write, "As Thomas Wolfe once said, 'You can't go home again'"? Yet no writer ever went home again with greater zest than Wolfe himself in his first novel, *Look Homeward, Angel*, published in 1929.

For generations of late-adolescent readers—mostly male, I suspect—the larger-than-life Gants of Altamont, North Carolina, mirrored their own families, however dissimiliar the factual details were, and young Eugene Gant's troubled love affair with his town and his parents mirrored their own fascination for what they most wanted to escape. And the prose, Wolfe's roaring, gushing, voluptuous torrent of language unlike anything heard outside one's own daydreams, seemed the way you should be expressing emotions if only you could get away with it.

The usual advice on Thomas Wolfe, of course, is that you should never re-read him. Remembered phrases, such as "O lost, and by the wind grieved, ghost, come back again," don't wear well or even make much sense (what do those commas around "ghost" mean?) 30 years later. But the old power is still there, and when it comes down to the end, when Eugene, bidding farewell to Altamont, is described as being "like a man who stands upon a hill above the town he has left, yet does not say 'The town is near,' but turns his eyes upon the distant soaring ranges," it is hard not to remember that wonderfully fearful excitement of leaving home.

—D. W. McC.

THE MAGIC CHRISTIAN

by Terry Southern - 1960

Mark down Terry Southern as Nathanael West's literary heir and "Grand Guy" Guy Grand as one of the most inspired satiric inventions since Miss Lonelyhearts. Guy Grand, the demented billionaire hero of *The Magic Christian*, spends tens of millions of dollars a year "making it hot" for people. Going into the big-car field, Grand makes a splash with a convertible longer and wider than the largest Greyhound bus. He enters a black panther in an international dog show. He makes it hot for British white hunters in the Congo by turning up with a 75-mm howitzer. He publishes a newspaper with a 2 million circulation filled with nothing but readers' opinions. His best practical joke, happily in the worst possible taste, is the launching of the luxury liner *Magic Christian*, followed by messages from the captain calculated to terrify his passengers. Published more than 25 years ago, *The Magic Christian* is still a very funny book.

—M. R.

THE MALTESE FALCON

by Dashiell Hammett - 1930

The Book-of-the-Month Club didn't take any notice of *The Maltese Falcon* when it was published in 1930. In fact, most respectable literary folk didn't. While British mysteries involving murders at the vicarage or devilish goings-on at the duke's annual masked ball had a certain intellectual chic, the homegrown product with its grubby private investigators and seedy roadhouse settings was ignored except by readers of fringe magazines such as *Black Mask*.

Dashiell Hammett changed all that. On page one of *The Maltese Falcon*, Effie, the secretary at the Spade and Archer detective agency, walks into her boss's office to announce Brigid O'Shaughnessy. Sam Spade looks up, says, "Yes, sweetheart?" and American literature is never quite the same again. Serious critics soon caught up with *The Maltese Falcon*, and four years after its publication an edition of it was reissued in The Modern Library, the first detective novel to make it into that pantheon of respectability.

But respectability was not Hammett's great contribution. He gave the American mystery story a distinct sound—a deadpan, slightly florid cadence that would spill over into the mainstream of American fiction. After all, as Sam Spade observed while rounding up his suspects in *The Maltese Falcon*, "The cheaper the crook, the gaudier the patter."

—D. W. McC.

THE MAN WITH THE GOLDEN ARM

by Nelson Algren - 1949

Frankie Machine is a dealer with a monkey on his back—a phrase that would pass unnoticed in our own "post-hip" times but was quite a revelation when this book came out. *The Man with the Golden Arm* was a trailblazing novel, taking most of us on our first trip to the gaudy sewer of inner-city drugs, where those monkeys hang out waiting to pounce on you; and nobody has yet written it better, because nobody has ever known a city better than Nelson Algren knew Chicago. Frankie Machine's story is poignant enough as he sweats out, and tries ineffectually to kick, his morphine habit (acquired in a wartime hospital) and struggles to keep things going with his invalid wife, all the while looking over his shoulder to see if the cops are about to bust his poker game, which is his livelihood. Every time he seems to be getting ahead of his habit, life gives him another brutal kick in the head, sending him reeling back to it.

But Frankie's story is just one detail in a panorama of city horrors and freak shows. Division Street in Chicago is Algren's stage, along which strut and shamble bums and hookers and con men, and all the riffraff of a great city in hard times. One scene in particular has stuck in my head for over 30 years, as a tribute to Algren's graphicness and passion for the incongruous. Every day a certain dog drops in on the local saloon where he is treated to a saucer of beer. The guys watch its eyes as it slurps, and, sure enough, one day the eyes glaze over—and just like that the pooch has become an alcoholic, one of them, part of the brotherhood. Combined with Algren's next best book, *A Walk on the Wild Side*, this novel constitutes by far the most powerful down-and-out city writing America has yet produced.   —W. S.

THE MOUNTAIN LION

by Jean Stafford - 1947

At first glance *The Mountain Lion* seems to have all the features of a Bobbsey Twins adventure story for children. There are the young brother and sister, Ralph and Molly, not twins but close enough, who live with their widowed mother and two superior older sisters on a small southern California farm. The big event of the year for the younger children is the annual visit of their colorful grandfather, a wealthy Texas rancher who is an embarrassment to their mother with her affectations of New England gentility. They also have an uncle in Colorado on whose ranch the children spend many action-filled summers.

But this second novel by Jean Stafford, published in 1947 before sensitive tales of troubled childhoods were all that common, is not an adventure yarn. It is a stunningly clear-eyed, unsentimental story of two children's progress from childhood to adolescence, an emotional journey made successfully by one but not the other. They learn of death and adult duplicity (or simple indifference) and catch intimations of that blurred boundary between affection and love.

Most of us, I suspect, have had our fill of overly cute, overly pretentious, overly dramatized literary children. In Ralph and especially Molly the potential for tragedy in ordinariness has rarely been presented better or with less bluster. —D. W. McC.

THE MOVIEGOER

by Walker Percy - 1961

Walker Percy, to my mind, is the most elegant and fastidious of American novelists now at work. A sort of Southern Evelyn Waugh. His first novel, *The Moviegoer*, succeeded in the most difficult of tricks—it managed to be witty, even hilarious, about despair. It is the grimly funny story of a man, Binx Bolling, who finds reality not in life but in the movies. Bolling, a 29-year-old stockbroker in New Orleans, is cursed with an indifference to life until he becomes involved with his stepcousin Kate, under treatment for suicidal tendencies, and his half brother Lonnie, confined to a wheelchair and soon to die. In this strange but beautiful story nothing is stated, everything is implied. The novel's revelations are set against New Orleans during Mardi Gras, an ambiance that is caught exactly.

The publication of *The Moviegoer*, which won the National Book Award in 1962, announced a major, if somewhat quirky, talent, very much to my taste. I always look forward to reading anything that Walker Percy writes.

—M. R.

THE NAKED AND THE DEAD

by Norman Mailer - 1948

This is the novel that launched Norman Mailer's career—his first full-length work of fiction. It was hailed at once as the most distinguished American novel about World War II. Too long, said some critics; unnecessarily repetitious, said others. But almost without exception they saw it as a profoundly moving account of an American platoon's invasion of a Japanese-held island, its struggle against the defenders' counterattack, and the final taking of the island. The book presents a gallery of Americans, from the rich major general to a poor Texas Mexican, and the action includes a night attack, a drunken soldier's seeking for souvenirs among the dead, and a climactic ascent of a mountain. By the end the secret drama of each man has been revealed.

In the *Book-of-the-Month Club News* John P. Marquand cited, among other aspects of the novel, a striking innovation in American letters: "a larger vocabulary of plain and fancy four-letter words than I have ever seen in print." He added, however, that the officers' and enlisted men's language is "the correct language of camp and beachhead." Today that language seems mild, but its use at the time was brave and vigorous.

—J. H.

NICKEL MOUNTAIN

by John Gardner - 1973

When novels and short stories by John Gardner began appearing in the 1960s there was always the question, since there were at least two other John Gardners turning out books, of which John Gardner he was. By the time *Nickel Mountain* was published in 1973 the confusion was over—there was no mistaking this John Gardner for anyone else. He once called all his books imitations, pointing out that *Nickel Mountain* was not an innocent novel but an imitation of an innocent novel. What he had in mind, he hinted, was something darker than it seemed. The message of the novel, it seems to me, falls somewhere between "Ain't love grand?" and "Ain't love weird?," the underlying premise being that just because people fall in love with the damnedest people doesn't mean they aren't really in love.

The setting is the Catskill Mountains—the upper, deeper Catskills that tourists have yet to discover. Henry Soames is the obese owner of the Stop-Off diner, who, more out of kindness than good sense, marries his young waitress, Callie, after she becomes pregnant and her rich boyfriend runs out on her. As the years go by and the two of them raise Callie's son as their own, they do indeed fall in love. Gardner subtitled the book "A Pastoral Novel," and, simply written and simply told, it has the sly power of a folktale.

—D. W. McC.

OTHER VOICES, OTHER ROOMS

by Truman Capote - 1948

Early in Truman Capote's first novel a truck driver takes a look at 13-year-old Joel Knox: "Radclif eyed the boy over the rim of his beer glass, not caring much for the looks of him. He had his notions of what a 'real' boy should look like, and this kid somehow offended them. He was too pretty, too delicate and fair-skinned. . . ." The description goes on to mention "girlish tenderness" and brown hair "streaked with pure yellow strands," but by that point most readers in 1948 had probably turned to the book's jacket to take another look at the photograph of the author, a languid figure sprawled on a fancy French couch, a young man of 23 who seemed to look a lot like that truck driver's estimation of Joel.

Those readers were looking at what is probably the most famous author's picture even taken. (The photographer, by the way, was Halma.) In a time before late-night talk shows and before the phrase "coming out of the closet" was ever uttered let alone thought, Capote's photograph led many readers who suspected that you could indeed judge a book by its cover to discover in *Other Voices, Other Rooms* a darkly lyrical novel of growing up in a tiny Southern town. It was a novel dealing with the discovery of sexuality, if not sex itself, that suggested a dimension of childhood not covered by Mark Twain or Booth Tarkington. They were also discovering the first major work by one of post-World War II America's most polished stylists, a writer whose orginality and sophistication would be dazzling readers for years to come.

—D. W. McC.

THE POSTMAN ALWAYS RINGS TWICE

by James M. Cain - 1934

Too many people know James M. Cain only from the movies that have been made from his novels—*The Postman Always Rings Twice, Double Indemnity, Mildred Pierce*—rather than from the books themselves. He has had rare good luck with the Hollywood versions of his novels, partly because the books themselves are designed along such clean, uncluttered lines. But the novels are better, and *Postman*, published in 1934, is probably the best of the lot.

"They threw me off the hay truck about noon," is how it begins. Not a word wasted as a drifter named Frank Chambers wanders into Twin Oaks Tavern, Nick Papadakis, proprietor, right along the highway just 20 miles from Los Angeles. On page two he meets Nick's wife, Cora, back in the kitchen washing dishes. A dozen pages later Frank and Cora have made love and are planning Nick's murder.

There is a mistaken notion that Cain is a suspense writer of the hard-boiled school. He rightly claimed that he never wrote a mystery in his life. Neither is he much interested in the sociological reasons why his Depression-weary characters live the way they do. They act with the directness of a kiss that turns into a bite. He tells their story. It's as simple, and as seemingly artless, as that.

Cain, a former newspaper reporter who had some experience as a Hollywood screenwriter, once said that you could always spot a B picture because the characters all "act too smart." It's a mistake he never made. In *Postman* no one acts any smarter than he should.

—D. W. McC.

RABBIT, RUN

by John Updike - 1960

The last sentence of *Rabbit, Run*, which is written entirely in the present tense, is simply, "Runs." "His hands lift of their own and he feels the wind on his ears even before, his heels hitting heavily on the pavement at first but with an effortless gathering out of a kind of sweet panic growing lighter and quicker and quieter, he runs. Ah: runs. Runs." That is the image of the dark side of the sunny Eisenhower 1950s. Harry (Rabbit) Angstrom, former high school basketball star now—at 26—salesman for a household gadget called Magipeel, running away, running from his life, from his vaguely alcoholic wife, from an accidentally killed baby and a pregnant girlfriend.

Rabbit, Run was John Updike's second novel, published in 1960, and it firmly established that his dazzling prose style was not the fluke of one short novel and a few short stories. It is a style seen best early in the novel when Rabbit stops to play a fast pickup game of basketball with some teenage boys and feels a rush of exhilaration but also a heaviness, a slowness, a sense of age that hadn't been in his memories of golden high school games.

But there is far more to the novel than stylistic grace. Rabbit may be a hollow man, but he is the hollow man of his generation. His memories are becoming shopworn, his emotional desires more compulsive. For him to face up to reality is to face up to seemingly hopeless failure. And when the Episcopalian minister comes to offer solace he offers it in the form of a good game of golf.

—D. W. McC.

RAGTIME

by E. L. Doctorow - 1975

In the *Book-of-the-Month Club News*, a reviewer (myself) said of E. L. Doctorow's volume that he couldn't recall a novel quite like this one. I still can't. Here is an uninhibited documentary in which certain memorable figures of the time mingle with various imagined characters to create in fable form a history of American life from the turn of the century to World War I. Here are such famous figures of the time as Harry Houdini, Henry Ford, Sigmund Freud, J. P. Morgan, Emma Goldman and Booker T. Washington. Here is a modest New Rochelle, New York, family that enters into the life of that era, fact and fiction mingling imaginatively and symmetrically in what, as the title suggests, is a ragtime rhythm. This two-decade kaleidoscope is a poetic innovation and that rare literary event, an original. —J. H.

THE RECOGNITIONS

by William Gaddis - 1955

That some literary failures or semi-failures are more interesting than many literary successes is a truism. Take the case of William Gaddis's first novel, *The Recognitions*. Today, for all its faults, it is considered a landmark in American avant-garde writing of the past three decades.

It's inordinately long (956 pages), at times exhibitionistic in its erudition, turgid, obscure, and in general its reach exceeds its grasp. But the reach is there—an ambition to create something like a total vision of what is false, forged, faked, in our 20th-century condition. The dimensions are large, the tone is at once serious and witty, the landscape far from pleasing. Unrestrained, yes, but that is sometimes inevitable in young writers of high energy.

In any case, *The Recognitions* has managed to last. It is approaching the stature of a persistent, underground classic. —C. F.

SEIZE THE DAY

by Saul Bellow - 1956

I'm not so foolish as to try to pick the best of Saul Bellow, obviously a major talent, because just about everything he has written is wonderful. Some of my friends swear by *Henderson the Rain King* as his most original work, and others have argued passionately for *The Adventures of Augie March* or *Mr. Sammler's Planet*. The truth is, you can't go wrong with any of these—or with *The Victim*, for that matter. But my favorite, after all these years, is still *Seize the Day*, the comic yet incredibly moving story of a middle-aged failure, Tommy Wilhelm.

Wilhelm, an unemployed salesman, lives in the same New York residential hotel as his father, a retired physician who despises him. Searching for work, he has dropped his last $700 in a loopy investment in the commodities market, made at the insistence of the seedy Dr. Tamkin. Wilhelm has a bruising final argument with his father, his estranged wife is threatening to sue him for nonsupport. His life is in ruins. Then he accidentally passes a funeral parlor and the sight of an unknown dead man makes him weep his heart out, suggesting that regeneration is possible.

These, mind you, are merely the bare story bones of what is a virtuoso performance. A funny, brilliant, profound novel by one of the few unarguably great writers of our time.　　　—M. R.

THE SHELTERING SKY

by Paul Bowles - 1949

T he composer and writer Paul Bowles and his gifted wife, Jane
Bowles, left the United States for Tangier in the late 1940s and
became perhaps our most famous expatriate writers following the
demise of the Lost Generation. This gripping novel evokes com-
parisons to the work of Samuel Beckett and Albert Camus, but
Bowles's existentialist Americans have a cast of their own. Port, a
well-to-do American, prides himself on being a "traveler" rather than
a mere "tourist," and he and his wife, Kit, have spent the 12 years of
their marriage making extended visits to foreign places. Now they
arrive in North Africa to travel into the Sahara. They bring along a
handsome young American, Tunner, whom Kit hopes will in some
way alter the growing estrangement between Port and herself.
Though they no longer share a bedroom, each is intensely bound to
the other. Port sometimes feels he exists only if Kit is thinking of him.
Kit feels the same about Port.

Bowles hauntingly renders the beauty of the exotic Arab and
African world, dominated always by the fierce sky, which Port con-
stantly observes in its changing state. For him, it is one of his few
certainties, for he feels it shelters us from the terrible void of nothing-
ness that he imagines lies on the other side.

As the three progress to more and more primitive, fly-ridden
towns, the relations between the three characters become more
complex. Tunner seduces Kit, and Port visits a beautiful young
prostitute. But both Kit and Port struggle to find their way back to the
core of their love for each other. Port shakes off Tunner to be alone

with Kit, but he contracts typhoid fever and lies in mortal danger in a small French outpost where he will eventually confront what does lie behind the phenomenon of human existence. And Kit, in a state of shock, kidnapped and imprisoned in a harem, will also come to "the end of the line," as the novel finally concludes in its last line. Bowles weaves a hypnotic tension, and despite the bleakness of the main characters' obsessions, the book itself is never bleak.   —G. N.

SLAUGHTERHOUSE-FIVE

by Kurt Vonnegut, Jr. - 1969

It seems in retrospect as if Kurt Vonnegut had spent the whole first half of his career preparing to write this book. As an American prisoner of war in Germany, he was present at the infamous fire-bombing of Dresden ("a terrible thing for the son of an architect to see"), but then words failed him for the next 20 years or so. Vonnegut passed the time by alternately polishing his gifts as a fantasist (*The Sirens of Titan*) and as a more or less straight novelist (*Mother Night*) until he felt ready to combine the two in this climactic thunderclap of a novel.

The straight novelist records with gruesome fidelity the brief army career of one Billy Pilgrim, who finds himself trapped and lost in the snow somewhere behind German lines during the Battle of the Bulge. He stumbles about for hours or years (he can't be sure) in frostbitten shock, gets captured and systematically reduced to a vege-table, and in *that* condition, witnesses the bombing.

When the smoke clears, Billy is faced with only one problem: how to live with the experience for the rest of his life? And here the fantasist steps in just in time to save Billy's sanity, with what now might be known as Dr. Vonnegut's special patent medicine—a good dream imposed on a bad one. Even as he is fighting a complete mental breakdown, Billy dreams his way onto the magical planet of Tralfamadore, where, among other blessings, there are no tenses, so that for all he knows he may have *always* been there. Thus when his mind drifts back to Dresden, the memory of it is broken up and made bearable by Tralfamadorian interludes, spent, among other things, in the kindly arms of a certain Montana Wildhack.

Kurt Vonnegut has been called an escapist, but nobody ever faced the horrors of life more squarely than he does in this book. His message, never more purely delivered, is that if those horrors are about to break you, you'd be a damn fool *not* to escape.

—W. S.

SONG OF SOLOMON

by Toni Morrison - 1977

The publication of *Song of Solomon*, a magnificent novel, was a cause for celebration. *Song of Solomon* is beautiful, funny, enormously moving, enchanting, laden with cunningly wrought mysteries. It is the best novel of the black experience in America since *Invisible Man*.

If I may interject a personal note, we on the Book-of-the-Month Club's Editorial Board do a good deal of reading. We try to approach each book afresh. With appetite. But sometimes (to come clean) it's difficult. The words fly in, the words fly out. *Song of Solomon* was something else. From the opening pages I sat bolt upright, aware that I was in the presence of a major talent. Toni Morrison had composed a fable that was everything that *Roots* was supposed to be but wasn't.

Ostensibly *Song of Solomon* is about grindingly poor blacks trapped in the slums of Detroit, and about other seemingly ignorant blacks, even more penurious, vegetating in the backwoods of Virginia. And yet—and yet—one emerges from the other end of this magical book envying the characters for their way of seeing, the texture of their experience, and the beauty of the legend of Milkman's great-grand-father, Solomon. Solomon, torn from Africa; Solomon, who, finding no escape from slavery possible, mounts a hill in Virginia, flaps his arms, and flies away home.

> *Solomon done fly, Solomon done gone*
> *Solomon cut across the sky, Solomon gone home.*

Toni Morrison is a writer who did much more than bring us news of another world. She altered our perception of the black experience.

—M. R.

THE SOUND AND THE FURY

by William Faulkner - 1929

"Through the fence, between the curling flower spaces, I could see them hitting. They were coming toward where the flag was and I went along the fence." So go the famous first two sentences of the novel that remained William Faulkner's own favorite and that introduce the world as seen through the eyes of the idiot Benjy. No American had written like Faulkner before, with his convoluted, idiosyncratic prose and challenging innovations of unexplained time jumps and nonsequential memories of the Compson family. Still, critics paid heed, and one placed him in the league of those other innovators, Proust and Joyce, though maintaining—accurately— that Faulkner was an American original.

Of the three voices that tell in turn most of the story—the idiot Benjy, his intellectual brother Quentin and the crass brother Jason— I've always been most held not by the childlike Benjy or the doomed Quentin but by Jason, the grasping hardware-store clerk who speaks in a forceful country speech that is often comic. Jason's bitter, self-righteous denunciations of New York stockbrokers and his profligate family and his desperate backroads pursuit of his niece, who runs off with a showman, lighten the story of family decline with savage comedy and make me cackle page after page. Like Proust and Joyce, Faulkner was concerned with time and memory, and for me this novel puts the writer from Oxford, Mississippi, up there with the writers from Paris and Dublin. —G. N.

STUDS LONIGAN

by James T. Farrell - 1932, 1934, 1935

T his trilogy of novels about Studs Lonigan announced to the literary world more than half a century ago that in James T. Farrell it had the author of a masterpiece. The novels include *Young Lonigan, The Young Manhood of Studs Lonigan* and *Judgment Day*, to which Farrell later added an epilogue. The trilogy has about it the finality of a sociological history: Chicago's Irish-American South Side in the late 1920s and early 1930s, crime-ridden, despairing, hopeless. Young Studs's mother wants him to be a priest, and Studs periodically reforms. But the gangster is the ideal among his South Side gang, and as he matures, Studs vacillates between being a tough guy, playing the horses and professing his love for a respectable young woman. By *Judgment Day*, Studs, at 29, has lost much of his youthful charm and energy, and is engulfed in a desperate escape into dance halls, movies and horse races as the Depression overtakes him.

Time has proved that the trilogy was more than just a vivid period portrait. The books endure because Farrell created in Studs a character who insists on being remembered. He is the street kid whose heart is good, whose mind is imaginative, whose soul wants him to be happy and loving, yet whose decline and death are tragically inevitable because of the milieu in which he has grown up. This is a work that rings with the grief and truth of a classic. —J. H.

THE SUN ALSO RISES

by Ernest Hemingway - 1926

"Red, a fellow's only got so many books like that in him." The speaker is Ernest Hemingway, the listener is Red Smith, and the subject is the book we're talking about right now. From our present vantage point we can only be mighty grateful that he had at least that one in him. When *The Sun Also Rises* came out in 1926, it seemed to be just what the phrase suggests: the dawn of a dazzling, incalculable new career. Later on the dawn turned out to be the best part of the day. But it was enough. This book has all the familiar Hemingway virtues, plus one that the author lost immediately after writing it: the freedom to be himself, or whatever else he chose. The novel made him a legend almost immediately, after which the legend pretty much told him what to do and how to write.

For instance, it seems unlikely that the later Hemingway would have dared to make his hero Jake Barnes sexually impotent, a "central observer" more passive even than one of Henry James's. But this device effectively decentralizes the novel, so that for once we have a whole roomful of people who are neither Hemingway nor mirrors of Hemingway. His powers of social observation in this novel are so acute, unsparing and plain funny that it's a mystery, and maybe a tragedy, that he used them so seldom thereafter. Here they permit him to skewer, like butterflies, a whole generation, mockingly called "lost"—the "sports" of several nations who romped through Europe in the 1920s having fun and casually destroying themselves and anyone else they ran into. Hemingway's touch is exquisite, all truth and no (visible) satire. The fun the young people are having is real fun—up to a point—whether it be running with the bulls or drinking oneself stiff, and the destruction is no worse than it probably was.

The shock that this novel caused had nothing to do with sensationalism. It must have been more like watching a window shade snap up sharply on a scene that no one had ever looked at so directly, or intelligently, or in bright sunlight, before. —w. s.

TALES OF THE CITY
(THE SERIES)*

by Armistead Maupin - 1978-1989

Armistead Maupin has been compared to Charles Dickens, Wilkie Collins, E. F. Benson, P. G. Wodehouse, and Evelyn Waugh, among others. All of these are appropriate, yet it's odd that we must turn to the British to find antecedents for a writer whose work seems so deeply rooted in contemporary American culture. One reason for this may be that, like Victorian novelists, Maupin wrote most of his novels in serial form (only the last in the series, *Sure of You*, did not first appear serialized in the *San Francisco Chronicle*). And another may be that Maupin's setting is San Francisco, that most European of American cities, with its steep hills so unlike New York or Chicago and its painstakingly maintained Victorian houses.

Yet there's nothing Victorian about the sensibility that Maupin expertly captures in his six-volume cycle. Beginning in the mid-1970s and continuing through the end of the 1980s, Maupin chronicles the lives of the post-Vietnam generation, still reeling from Watergate, trying to make sense of what the sexual revolution has wrought (in the city that practically invented the sexual revolution) and, later, trying to cope with the devastation of AIDS (in the American city that was perhaps more devastated than any other by AIDS). One can only wonder about the variety of social

---

*Tales of the City / More Tales of the City / Further Tales of the City / Babycakes / Significant Others / Sure of You

circles Maupin traveled in, for he serves up deliciously accurate portraits of freeze-dried hippies, unreconstructed male chauvinists, feminists and feminazis, tradition-bound socialites, captains of industry, closeted and openly gay men, clergymen, the homeless, and just about everything in between. The panoply of characters, coupled with the wild twists and turns of Maupin's plotlines (expertly and intricately interwoven, again in the manner of several Victorian novelists), leaves us with the impression that in San Francisco, anything can and probably will happen.

San Franciscans apparently devoured Maupin's columns as they appeared, often trying to discern the sometimes thinly-veiled role models for some of his characters and anticipating what fun he would have with various local scandals. At one point Maupin includes a Cervantes-like self-reference to that "columnist" who sets tongues wagging. But if Maupin's series was only commentary on provincial, contemporaneous events, however entertaining, it wouldn't enjoy its nationwide popularity, and it wouldn't seem as vivid, hilarious, poignant, and bittersweet today as the first book did twenty years ago.

For all his topicality and pop culture references, Maupin is not at heart a political writer or social chronicler. He's a humanist and a born storyteller. In fifty years time references to Patty Hearst, Tricia Nixon Cox, and TAB may lose their resonance and nostalgia value, but the residents of 28 Barbary Lane, presided over by the aptly-named Anna Madrigal, the most wonderful landlady anyone could hope for, will remain a group of people readers will delight in discovering. For all his similarities to various British authors with the same wicked wit and gift for sharp social observation, Maupin's real concern remains that most American of subjects: how we continuously invent and reinvent ourselves, our families, and our communities.   —M. M. M.

TENDER IS THE NIGHT

by F. Scott Fitzgerald - 1934

Tender Is the Night has always suffered the fate of being compared to its handsome little brother, *The Great Gatsby*. Outside of the author's name, there is no serious comparison. *Gatsby* is short and perfect, and—at least in the case of books—it's a lot easier to be perfect if you're short. *Tender* is big, rich and, all right, flawed. F. Scott Fitzgerald poured so much of himself into it that he couldn't always keep the shape straight, and his lyrical prose sometimes bursts into lushness. These are minor offenses in view of the book's achievements, because Fitzgerald also pulls off the near-impossible: he manages to translate his own private torments with Zelda and alcohol into a totally convincing fable about two quite different people.

The story concerns a brilliant psychologist who saves a patient from madness, falls in love with her and pours his strength into her, only to lose both her and his strength. It is all so authentically *felt* that a psychiatrist friend of mine used to read the book once a year and imagine himself into the soul of Dr. Dick Diver and wind up doing crazy tricks on an actual diving board to prove he hadn't lost his strength after all. And it's a rare novel that can do that to *anyone*.

But the Divers' story represents more than just one man's crack-up. Fitzgerald also gives us perhaps the best portrait we have of a whole doomed community: the fun-loving expatriates of the '20s, still frolicking gamely on the Riviera in the shadow of Depression and war. By following his rich patient-wife into that world, Dick Diver has bought into both the fun and the doom. In a haunting climactic scene the once-masterful doctor winds up bestowing a boozy papal blessing over the crowd on the beach before departing alone for the United States. Fitzgerald, who had once celebrated the decade and who helped to invent it, is telling us, and himself, that the party is over. —W. S.

THEM

by Joyce Carol Oates - 1969

This powerful novel traces the violent lives of a blue-collar family struggling for survival in the inner city of Detroit. In the late 1930s, Loretta's first lover is murdered in her own bed by her unstable brother, and the young woman is forced into marriage with a weak, silent man. Loretta is occasionally bold and lucky, more often impetuous and destructive. Over the next 30 years, she and her 3 children—the handsome, daring Jules, shy Maureen and rebellious Betty—succumb to different fates in their harsh world on the fringes of American prosperity, a brutal culture marked by male violence, continuing poverty and the clear advantage of crime over law-abiding life. The father is killed in a horrifying steel-mill accident, and Jules virtually leaves home to pursue a nomadic life on the streets, occasionally returning with money. Maureen, the good girl, is abused by Loretta and her second husband, and, feeling deserted by her beloved brother, abandons her dutiful, parochial-school existence for quick pickups by middle-class men. Jules, involved with a rich swindler, falls into a passionate affair with a wealthy Grosse Pointe girl who briefly runs away with him.

Loretta alternately abuses and protects her children and often suffers violence from her ill-chosen men. Only Maureen will escape into a middle-class life, though she will remain haunted and obsessed by her family's nightmare lives. The novel culminates in the Detroit riots of 1967 when the have-nots arise against the haves in an orgy of arson, looting, murder and revenge.

Ms. Oates reveals that the novel is based on the actual recollections

74

of a young woman she taught in Detroit. Two of the author's recurrent themes—violence and personal disintegration—credibly animate this complex work that gives us a portrait of a large segment of American society. Just as Theodore Dreiser's *Sister Carrie* showed how easy it was for city dwellers of an earlier day to slip through the cracks of life, *them* shows how similar forces work today. Terrifying at times, the novel is more terrifying for not having dated in the nearly 20 years since its publication. Indeed, as more Americans sink into unemployment, it provides an eerie vision of what may lie in store as more of "us"—the believers in the American Dream—become "them."   —G. N.

TO KILL A MOCKINGBIRD

by Harper Lee - 1960

Harper Lee's first novel was bold for its time, a passionate appeal for racial justice in a Deep South town where violence was taken for granted and too often went unpunished. It is still a gripping tale. Its narrator, "Scout" Finch, the six-year-old daughter of a brave, liberal lawyer, artfully tells a story with a child's simplicity. The story involves the unjust conviction of a black man for the rape of a white woman, his defense by Scout's father, the murder of the prisoner when he tries to escape from a prison camp and the effort of the woman's poor-white father to destroy the lawyer's children. How they are saved is the cleverly plotted climax of a somber tale that also has a considerable share of good humor. This was one of the few first novels to win a Pulitzer Prize, a salute with which only a diehard redneck could have found fault. —J. H.

THE TRANSIT OF VENUS

by Shirley Hazzard - 1980

M any book people treasure a short list of novels they think of as unappreciated. *The Transit of Venus*, Shirley Hazzard's third novel, appears on mine. It is herewith recommended to readers attuned to the delicacies and elegancies of the Henry James school. Cunningly constructed to surprise or trip up the over-casual reader, *The Transit of Venus* deals with 30 years in the lives of two Australian sisters living in London, the vivid Caro and the tamer Grace. Even more memorable is the portrait of their ineffable (and intolerable) half sister, Dora: Ms. Hazzard can be hard on her own sex.

Perceptive, beautifully written, *Transit*, it seems to me, deserves a wider readership. —C. F.

THE TREES/THE FIELDS/ THE TOWN

by Conrad Richter - 1940, 1946, 1950

This remarkable trilogy about the growth of an Ohio settlement is not one of those traditional historical dramas in which the hero miraculously bumps into George Washington on a surveying trip in the woods or overhears a conversation between Benjamin Franklin and another Founding Father. Conrad Richter's interest was not in the large historical incidents. Rather, his people—whose idiomatic speech he produces with rare accuracy—are heroic and human characters who show what it was really like for Americans forging into the forbidding wilderness and how they slowly imposed settlement on the American frontier.

At the heart of the story is Sayward Luckett, a strapping young woman whose father is an example of the "woodsy," distrusting towns and often away by himself on hunting trips in the wilderness. Sayward assumes responsibility for her sisters and brother when their mother dies. She is a feisty young woman capable of drowning a deer for food when the family is starving. Throughout her long life she will show strength and resilience, whether meeting tragedy, joy or the absurdities of fate. When she decides to marry she settles on an older Easterner named Portius Wheeler who is tricked into marriage while drunk. Their marriage will not be smooth, as Portius's admiration for order and Yankee civilization conflicts with Sayward's rustic experience. Her siblings and her children encounter all manner of experience—death, love triangles, kidnapping by Indians and eventually prosperity, the family finally acquiring a mansion in the new town.

Anyone who wants to feel what life was like when America was being settled—the silence of the wilderness, the courage of isolated families—should start here. 　　　　　　　　　　　—G. N.

U.S.A. (THE 42ND PARALLEL, 1919, THE BIG MONEY)

by John Dos Passos - 1930, 1933, 1936

No novelist has attempted to write about the United States with such a panoramic view as John Dos Passos in this trilogy of novels. Stretching from 1898 to the Depression '30s, these technically innovative novels portray an extraordinary cross-section of people, economic conditions and politics. Dos Passos splices together three main elements: "newsreels" that document the headlines, songs and scandals of the time—a moving tabloid of what the man in the street was experiencing; capsule biographies of inventors, radicals, movie stars and financiers who shaped the new society; and more than 10 major characters who ricochet up and down the social ladder pursuing success, money or meaning. Who can forget the flying ace Charley Anderson, a Lindbergh-like figure whose youthful promise shrinks as he succumbs to booze, grasping women and bad business schemes? Or Mac, a poor and decent Irish kid who becomes radicalized while riding the rails with other unemployed men and joins the labor fight? Or J. Ward Moorehouse, another poor boy who turns himself into a smooth-lying king of public relations and advertising, or liberal Mary French, who loses her communist boyfriend to Moscow, or Margo Dowling, who parlays a dismal childhood into movie stardom?

Dos Passos seems to know every street of every American city, as well as the dynamics of big business, labor radicalism and low and high society. His deterministic vision of Americans, caught up in our society's economic machinery, made him unfashionable with later critics, but his trilogy stands up as monumental.　　　—G. N.

THE WALL

by John Hersey - 1950

A vast and varied Holocaust literature is one of the results of the systematic murder by the Nazis of 6 million Jewish men, women, children and babies waiting to be born. Amid this torrent of testimony, notable works of imagination, naturally enough, are not too often encountered. Surely one of them is John Hersey's *The Wall*.

In November of 1939 the Germans took over the Warsaw ghetto. By May of 1943 they had completed their masterwork: the ghetto and its people were no more. Using the notes and diary of one Noach Levinson as a structural device (and doubtless drawing upon actual surviving documents), Mr. Hersey wrote in 1950 (it was a BOMC Selection) a fictional interpretation of this black chapter of history. Distilling the realistic atmosphere of a documentary, *The Wall* endures as a tribute to the capacity of the human spirit to meet and at times to triumph over the last extremity of human baseness.

Today, at a time when many powerful voices are urging us to "forget it," *The Wall* compels us still to remember.   —C. F.

THE WAPSHOT CHRONICLE

by John Cheever - 1957

In one of John Cheever's short stories he catalogues—and parodies—a list of clichéd characters and plots that won't appear in his next novel or anything else he would write. One of them involves a mysteriously chic international cast whose trans-European train is trapped by an avalanche. He dismisses the situation by asking, "How could this snowy and trumped-up pass, with its trio of travelers, hope to celebrate a world that lies spread out around us like a bewildering and stupendous dream?"

That is the best description I've seen of just what John Cheever does as a writer, and the key word is "celebrate." He celebrates a world as bewildering and as stupendous and as utterly ordinary as suburban Westchester, both with its commuters and its inmates at Sing Sing prison, and small-town New England, with its faded illusions of gentility. Nowhere did he do it better or with such élan than in his first novel, *The Wapshot Chronicle*, published in 1957.

The Wapshots—complete with an unsuccessful father, a practical mother, an eccentric matriarchal aunt and two steadily maturing sons—live in St. Botolphs, a Massachusetts seaport that has seen better days. In the course of their chronicle they encounter love and lust and death. It is a wise and very funny book, a combination that is rarer than it should be. —D. W. McC.

WHAT MAKES SAMMY RUN?

by Budd Schulberg - 1941

Any novelist who has added a new name to the language has done, in essence, what every novelist strives to do: he has identified a new species and, like Adam in the Garden, he has found the perfect name, the right sound, for it. As soon as Sammy Glick appeared, we seemed to know a hundred of him. Sammy is the all-American hustler, a guy who plays life as if it were the Roller Derby, all flying hips and elbows and whatever it takes. Starting out as a newspaper copy boy, he rises to the top of the movie business by a daunting mixture of flattery, plagiarism and backstabbing worthy of the Borgias. Yet he retains a curious innocence: this is the way you had to do it on the Lower East Side, this is the way you do it now. His father was a saintly failure, and to hell with that. The rest of the world consists, in his eyes, either of suckers like his old man, or of lesser Sammy Glicks, who just don't do it as well as he does. When he gets to Hollywood, he doesn't find anything he hasn't seen before—except for luxury and table manners, which he has a comical time with at first. Otherwise he plays it exactly like the old neighborhood, with the same profitable results, and even ends up as the perfect ersatz Hollywood gentleman.

Budd Schulberg was born and raised in the movie business, and he knows better than any writer before or since how the original Hollywood was created by gamblers (it had to be, respectable bankers wouldn't touch it), and how the gamblers, on close inspection, form an uncanny group portrait of Sammy Glick.　　　　—W. S.

WHEAT THAT
SPRINGETH GREEN*

by J. F. Powers - 1988

L ike many of the novels I cherish, this once seemed like an unlikely choice. I can't remember what attracted me to it, but my battered copy of the ten-year-old hardcover testifies to the number of times I've urged other people to borrow and read this book. *Wheat That Springeth Green* is a comedy about the distance between the ideals of youth and the realities of existence, with no easy answers but a lot of tantalizing clues as to where the author stands. The story's hero, Joe Hackett, is a priest in suburban Minnesota. Back in his seminary days, he seemed on track to become an intellectual or spiritual superstar, or both. Instead, he's ended up a workaday priest. People in the novel are divided about whether or not Joe's any good as a parish priest; whether he's achieving his spiritual goals is a different question, but the external evidence isn't promising. His manner is curmudgeonly. He can't seem to disguise his disappointment in the human race. In the rectory he unwinds by watching old movies and Twins games on TV and drinking, too much drinking. Has he lost his way? It looks that way, but Powers is a master of comic surprise, and of transforming the story in a way the reader (this reader) would never predict. The priesthood is a sack race, Joe tells a young curate who can't understand his way of doing things. Not a 100-yard dash, not a mile run. What Joe means by this, and what J. F. Powers means by this, should be experienced, not summarized.   —L. S.

---

*The title is taken from a medieval carol: "Now the green blade riseth from the buried grain, wheat that in dark earth many days has lain; love lives again, that with the dead has been: Love is come again like wheat that springeth green."

THE WORLD ACCORDING TO GARP

by John Irving - 1978

It has been suggested that novelists, living in chaos like the rest of us, retaliate by composing ordered worlds of their own, proffering them as fictions. If that's the case, John Irving is a brilliant exception to the rule. What he has created in *The World According to Garp* is a zany novel of inspired anarchy. Some literary lightning. Something special for admirers of Nathanael West, Terry Southern and Joseph Heller. And yet refreshingly original.

This savagely comic novel thrives on many levels. It is a flinty satire—long overdue—of the more extreme reaches of the feminist movement. It is also a surprisingly sweet evocation of family life, the paranoia that springs from a man's concern for the safety of his wife and children. Or, put another way, Garp's hilarious but touching attempts to construct a kind of fort for his own family, where they can live "unmolested, even untouched by what is called 'the rest of life,'" are conspicuously unsuccessful. Yet for all its nicely calculated shocks, *The World According to Garp* can be savored as a cry of puritan outrage against mindless violence.

I can no more render a coherent outline of the plot of *The World According to Garp* than I could the story line of a Marx Brothers movie. Suffice it to say that where the latter leaves off, avoiding real offense, *Garp* merely begins. It is a novel that will offend some and infuriate others, and even though it would have benefited from some pruning, it delighted me. Garp, after he become a successful novelist, writes to a disgruntled reader: "I have nothing but sympathy for how people behave—and nothing but laughter to console them with.

Laughter is my religion. In the manner of most religions, I admit that my laughter is pretty desperate." Yes, and abusive as well, but redeemed by disarming tenderness and a large talent that announces itself on almost every page. —M. R.